MONOGRAPHIC JOURNALS OF THE NEAR EAST
SYRO-MESOPOTAMIAN STUDIES 5/1 (July 1991)
A publication of
IIMAS — The International Institute for Mesopotamian Area Studies

SMS 5/1

MOZAN 2

THE EPIGRAPHIC FINDS
OF THE SIXTH SEASON

Lucio Milano

with contributions by
Giorgio Buccellati, Marilyn Kelly-Buccellati, and Mario Liverani

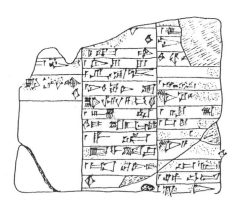

Malibu 1991
Undena Publications

The series *Monographic Journals of the Near East* includes medium size monographs, published independently of each other and without any periodical schedule. For convenience, they are grouped into volumes which are closed when a total of about 200 pages is reached. Individual titles are available on a standing order basis, which can be placed with the publisher for each of the various journals. – Beginning with 1991, the text portion of most monographs is available on disk in MS-DOS/ASCII format, within the series *Cybernetica Mesopotamica: Electronic Editions*, which is also distributed by Undena Publications.

General Editor: Giorgio Buccellati

The journal *Syro-Mesopotamian Studies* is devoted to the study of the civilizations which flourished in the area characterized by the use of Sumerian and Akkadian, from late prehistory to the end of the First Millennium B.C., providing an outlet for the publication of primary sources and a forum for the archaeological, linguistic and historical analysis of pertinent phenomena.

Editor: Marilyn Kelly-Buccellati

Assistant Editor: William R. Shelby

Advisory Board: Jean Bottéro
Giorgio Gullini
Thorkild Jacobsen
Olivier Rouault
Maurits Van Loon

SMS 5/1. – The tablets recovered in Mozan during the sixth season of excavations in 1990 represent the northernmost find to date of well stratified cuneiform texts for the third millennium. They are accounts of people listed by name, profession and sometimes provenience. The language in which the texts are written is plausibly Old Akkadian, and so is a majority of personal names, but several names may be explained as Hurrian. The date is that of the later portion of the Sargonic period. Besides providing a complete philological treatment of the texts, this fascicle briefly describes the archaeological context – a stratigraphically well defined deposit within a sizeable stone building; it also provides a brief report on the work of the sixth season of excavations.

An electronic version of the text portion of this monograph (labeled *CM E2*) is available from Undena.

Publication of this monograph was made possible through a grant from the National Endowment of the Humanities.

ISBN: 0-89003-276-9

Table of Contents

List of Figures

List of Illustrations

Numbers in brackets refer to the Mozan photo archive.

1. Introduction – G. Buccellati and M. Kelly-Buccellati

1.1 The sixth season of excavations at Tell Mozan

We present in this fascicle a brief preliminary report on the sixth season of excavations at Tell Mozan,[1] in which pride of place is given to the single most important find of that season – two cuneiform tablets of the latter part of the third millennium. As the second in our sequence of official excavation reports, this monograph deals first with the broader background of the sixth season as a whole; it also takes up is some detail the issue of the general archaeological and specific stratigraphic context in which the tablets are situated.

Excavations at Tell Mozan are made possible through grants from the National Endowment for the Humanities, the Ambassador International Cultural Foundation, the S. H. Kress Foundation, the Martin Foundation, Neutrogena Corporation, and various private donors. The Mozan Archaeological Project is under the overall sponsorship of IIMAS – The International Institute for Mesopotamian Area Studies, with the collaboration of the University of California, Los Angeles; California State University, Los Angeles; and the University of Rome.

[1]The sixth season lasted from April 30 to July 5, 1990. The staff included the following individuals: Marilyn Kelly-Buccellati and Giorgio Buccellati, directors; Sharyn L. Crane, assistant director and archaeologist; Mario Liverani, Antone J. Mathys, Barbara Cifola, Alessandra Asteriti, archaeologists; Stephen M. Hughey, surveyor and archaeologist; Lucio Milano epigraphist and archaeologist; Daniele Ghidoli, Patricia D. Kent and Federico A. Buccellati, photographers; Carla Pearson, Darlene A. Siedschlag and Kathy King, draftspersons; Suzanne Robey and Karen Nathan, registrars; Chiara Sogno Buccellati, conservator; Judith Thompson-Miragliuolo and Skia, palaeoecologists; Mark L. Peterson and David Miller, geophysicists; Bruno Marcolongo, geomorphologist; Jean Mathys, hydrologist; Peter Nathan, technical manager; Pamela Hughey, house manager. Messrs. Muhammad Muktash of the National Museum in Raqqa and Ali Ali of the Hassaka section of the Directorate General of Antiquities and Museums were the representatives of the Directorate General. Mr. Jean Lazar, Director of the Office in Hassaka, and his assistants, Mr. Ibrahim Nano and Ms. Najah Touer, were also particularly helpful during our season of excavations.

As always, we benefitted fully from the invaluable assistance of our hosts and colleagues in the Directorate General of Antiquities and Museums, both in Damascus and in Hassaka. We wish in particular to acknowledge the warm spirit of collegiality with which we were received by Dr. Ali Abu-Assaf, the new Director General. It was in fact a great pleasure for us that during our first season in Mozan since his taking the leadership of the Directorate General, he was able to accompany the Minister of Culture of the Syrian Arab Republic, Dr. Najah Attar, on a visit to the site, together with the Governor of the Province of Hassaka, Mr. Muhammad Mustafa Miro, and with Dr. Adnan Bounni, Director of Excavations. We are always mindful of the fact that if we have been able to a make a strong commitment to a long term and ambitious program of archaeological work in Syria it is due in large measure to the unqualified support that we have received over the years from the Syrian authorities, who have been unfailing in both providing every possible assistance in all practical needs and showing at the same time the greatest interest in our intellectual concerns. The official visit of the Minister and the Director General was in this respect especially symbolic coming as it did upon completion of our new Expedition House, which will allow us to implement a much more effective program of excavation and laboratory research over the coming years.

1.2 Archaeological objectives

A major objective of the sixth season was to open two new areas of excavation on the High Mound (see below, Fig.1), chosen from the particular perspective which we had gained in earlier seasons about the layout and occupation of the site. One of these areas was Area F, where we anticipated that we might be able to obtain a substantial horizontal exposure of strata dated to the earliest periods of the history of the site. The reason for this assumption was based on the results of our 1984 surface ceramic collection, and on the observation that here the gradient of the tell is not very steep, thus allowing for a fairly broad excavation unit situated by the toe of the slope. Work in this unit is described briefly below by M. Liverani.

A second new operation (labeled AS) was a stepped trench chosen for just the opposite reasons. The area in question corresponds to the highest rise on the the

High Mound, where our 1984 ceramic survey had resulted in the largest concentration of later material. Another important consideration for the choice of this area was its particular topographic configuration: its long and gradual slope followed the orientation of the city wall in a parallel line, rather than cutting across it at a perpendicular. The trench was so laid out that it followed the slope in this particular direction, ending in its lowest part with a fairly large and level area, not much higher in elevation than the level of the Outer City, but still well within the projected perimeter of the inner City Wall. Our expectation was to obtain thereby a complete stratigraphic sequence for the occupational history of the site, with the possibility of further horizontal excavation where the stratigraphy would warrant it. The results did indeed match very closely our expectations. From small private houses of the Nuzi period at the top, and through sizeable brickwork remains of the Khabur period, we came, about half way through the slope, to late third millennium strata, and began to excavate at the bottom of the trench a large structural complex of the mid third millennium, which appears to be a relatively well preserved public building. We are currently working on the publication of a preliminary monograph which will be devoted entirely to this trench.[2]

Two other major ancillary projects were brought to completion during the sixth season, and a third one was begun. The first two are a new topographical survey of the site, including a much finer coverage of the Outer City, and the geophysical survey, which had been started in 1988: a separate publication is being prepared for each of these projects, by S. M. Hughey and by J. Ericson and M. L. Peterson respectively. A geo-morphological survey of the immediate environs of the site was begun by B. Marcolongo, who also plans to continue his work at the site in 1992.

---

[2]We had also intended to complete, during the sixth season, the excavations of the Temple BA, but we were hampered by the fact that some key members of our projected staff were not able to join us in the field, so we had to postpone that particular operation. We intend to resume it in the 1992 season (since we are working on a two year cycle, according to the current policies of the Directorate General of Antiquities and Museums). Publication of the temple excavations is thus postponed until after that date. See for now *Mozan 1*, 59-61; *SAB 2*; Kelly-Buccellati 1990a; 1990b.

1.3 The epigraphic finds

The present monograph is devoted primarily to the epigraphic finds which were made in area F1 during the sixth season. We are especially grateful to Lucio Milano for the speed and competence with which he has prepared this material for publication. This find is clearly sufficiently important to warrant immediate publication in this form. To be sure, no one more than Milano himself is aware of the fact that the discovery of additional tablets may significantly increase our understanding of these documents; and given the fact that the tablets came from the very top layers of a deposit contained within a well preserved building, we may in fact expect that future excavations in this area may yield additional epigraphic finds of the same nature. Similarly, in spite of the relatively clear stratigraphic definition of the structural remains in F1, it is obvious, as Liverani emphasizes in his presentation below, that we may well expect a finer resolution as a result of an increased exposure.[3] In this sense, therefore, this is truly a preliminary report. And yet both the degree of definition which is already possible at this juncture, and the significance of the finds in themselves, are such that we felt immediate publication was needed within the official sequence of the Mozan reports.

The tablets published here represent the northernmost cuneiform epigraphic finds of the third millennium excavated to date.[4] Though not at a great distance from Tell Brak, Mozan appears to fit in a milieu rather different from Brak: hence the fact that the preponderance of names in our tablets are Akkadian, and even more importantly the fact that the tablets themselves were most probably written in Akkadian (as argued by Milano, below), is significant because it marks a stronger link with the south than one might at first have expected. Since the date of the tablets appears to be relatively late in the Sargonic period, we may have here evidence of the spreading of Akkadian cultural, and possibly also administrative, influence, suggesting perhaps that the Akkadian kings had suc-

---

[3]For instance, one wonders if the deposit in which the tablets were found (f73) is a levelling in function of a higher terrace, or a floor accumulation; or what the fuller stratigraphic connections might be between the "upstairs" and the "downstairs" strata; or again whether some details of the comparisons in ceramic typology may not have to be revised.

[4]See Fig. 7. The Naram-Sin inscription of Pir Hüseyn is the only one coming from a location even farther to the north, but this text was not found in an excavation, and doubts have been raised as to whether it was found in or even near its original emplacement, or was brought there in later times, see references cited in Börker-Klähn 1982, p.134.

ministrative, influence, suggesting perhaps that the Akkadian kings had succeeded in securing not only the lower funnel of the Khabur (where Brak was the major center), but also the upper plains in the piedmont region of Mozan.

The presence of Hurrian onomastic elements in our tablets is however even more significant. The case should not be overstated, because only one name (*Ú-na-ap-šè-ni*) can be matched as a full name in the later onomastic Hurrian repertory, while in the other cases we can only isolate individual onomastic elements (see Milano's comments below, 3.6 and 3.7). Nevertheless, our data do provide some meaningful new evidence for the presence of Hurrian linguistic elements in this region at this date. Conversely, the total absence of Amorite names provides a strong intimation as to the presumed absence of such a linguistic element. This is in line with the thesis advanced in *Mozan 1* as one of the research objectives of our excavations, to the effect that the Khabur plains were an early Hurrian enclave. What the overall influence of the Hurrian linguistic element may have been, how far back in time the Hurrian scribal tradition extended (first clearly attested in the Tiš-atal inscriptions), how widespread the Akkadian cultural and administrative presence was – these are clearly questions that cannot be answered at this stage. But the very fact that we can pose them in such detail is indicative of the significance of our epigraphic finds from 1990, and of the interest and determination with which we will pursue this particular set of problems in our future work at the site.

1.4 Notes on third millennium ceramic chronology at Mozan

The ceramics found in the two storerooms of Area F1 are consistent with those from other third millennium deposits excavated so far at Mozan, and yet sufficiently different to warrant a brief comparative discussion here. Through the sixth season (Spring 1990), we have excavated major deposits with a significant corpus of ceramics from: two burials in the Outer City (Oa4 and especially Ob1, where there were over 50 vessels found as part of a grave); the burnt deposit (f16) in Area K1 immediately outside the city wall; the Temple BA; and now the two storerooms in Area F1. In the Ob1 grave a substantial corpus of late Ninevite V vessels was found including the large pointed base, globular bowls with deeply grooved designs (Fig. 8e) also excavated at Tell Ailun west of Mozan and Tell

with geometric designs painted in red and black (Moortgat and Moortgat-Correns 1976, Abb. 28a,b) were placed in this tomb along with small, roughly made and poorly fired Metallic ware cups (Fig. 8a-d). As will be demonstrated in detail in the publication of this pottery, on which I am currently working, it appears that the contents were placed in this tomb at a point late in terms of the Ninevite V and Scarlet ware tradition (at least in our area) and early in the Metallic ware tradition. This then means that Ob1 represents the earliest third millennium deposit thus far excavated at Mozan. It is not, however, the earliest third millennium deposit extant at Mozan since surface sherds of earlier Ninevite V incised ceramics have been found. In fact it was especially this earlier material which gave us the impetus to excavate in Area F1 (see below 2.1).

Between this deposit and the next chronological segment of the pottery chronology there is probably a short gap since the city wall burnt deposit (f16) in Area K1 does not overlap with the material from the tombs. This, however, may also be due to the nature of the burnt deposit and the fact that a limited range of types was found there (*Mozan 1*, pp. 65-67). The ceramics from this burnt deposit are dated partly through comparison with other sites but also by the date of the seal impressions on the door sealings (*Mozan 1*, pp. 67-81). Storage vessels with plastered interiors and some of the Simple ware shapes overlap the ceramics found in Temple BA. Most of the ceramics from the Temple BA are from the Simple ware tradition but a significant proportion is Metallic ware. This is also true for the vessels in the storerooms in Area F1. Some overlap of types may be seen in the decorated storage vessels but confirmation of this awaits the restoration of the F1 material. Certainly both the Simple ware and the Metallic ware of these rooms are somewhat different in both shape and manufacturing technique from that of the wares excavated in Temple BA.[5]

Thus even at this preliminary stage we may propose that the F1 storage rooms are among the latest third millennium ceramic material excavated at Mozan. One of the goals of the Mozan excavation is to reconstruct a well articulated ceramic chronology for the third millennium through substantial deposits of well stratified material combining not only the ceramics but also their associated objects which

---

[5]A useful link for establishing the internal third millennium ceramic chronology at Mozan will probably be not so much the conical cups as in the south (see comment by Oates 1986, p. 272) but rather the Simple ware spouted vessels. Already we have a progression of types from the city wall through this new deposit in the F1 storerooms. In general, the earliest spouted vessels have short spouts attached to the shoulders of small, squat jars while the later examples have longer spouts on taller, somewhat larger jars.

material combining not only the ceramics but also their associated objects which can give independent evidence for the date of these deposits. The vessels found *in situ* in the two storerooms of Area F1 are an important step in this direction. If these storeroom vessels do indeed also turn out to be dated by the tablets published here, then we will have a secure anchor for the later part of the Sargonic period.

1.5 An inscribed sherd from the fifth season (M2 3)

By way of a complement to the tablets from F1, we also publish here a sherd inscribed with a few cuneiform signs which was found in 1988 during the fifth season of excavations. Discovered on the surface of the tell by J. Ericson during his work on the geo-physical survey, it came from the an area immediately west of the Temple BA. It was assigned the field number Z1.66, and is published here under the label **M2 3** (see Illustr. 6). To date, this is the only other epigraphic find demonstrably from Mozan.[6]

A reading of the few signs remains uncertain. The best interpretation is the one which has been offered privately by W. W. Hallo, whom we wish to thank for his kindness in sharing his insight with us. He suggests that the signs may be read as the logogram E_2.LUḪ,[7] possibly referring to a lustration establishment – which would fit with the fact that the findspot of the sherd happened to be near a temple, though this may of course be purely accidental.

---

[6]For our tentative suggestion that the Tiš-atal lions may also have been found at Mozan see *Mozan 1*, pp. 36-38.

[7]For a comparable sign which is "remotely similar" in shape to our second sign, Hallo (private communication) refers to a Kassite LUḪ listed in Fossey 1926 as # 19735. He also notes that the sign LUḪ may of course be read as SUKKAL, so that, "if the signs are read correctly, they can be interpreted as 'house of the messenger' as well as 'bath house,' 'house of lustration(s)' or the like." We conclude, as he does, with a sober *non liquet*.

2. The archaeological context – M. Liverani

2.1 General setting

During the 6th season in Tell Mozan (May-June 1990), a new operation was started in the Northern area of the mound (area F; operation F1; cf. Fig. 1).[8] The operation was carried on in squares of 5 by 5 meters in size, with no baulks, excavated in a checkered fashion in order to temporarily preserve the sections to be drawn. Four such squares were originally opened in order to obtain an area of 10 by 10 meters, eventually enlarged for practical needs to cover a total area of 10 by 12.50 meters (Fig. 2).

The area selected for excavation is located on the left (i.e. western) flank of an erosion gully leading northwards to the edge of the High Mound, sufficiently inside the mound to avoid meeting the interior of the city-wall. The absolute elevations of F1 (from ca. 489 to 486) are roughly mid-way between the top of the mound (area B is ca. 499-498) and the Outer City (ca. 480).

This area had been selected for excavation in the hope that the levels of the first half of the third millennium ("Ninevite 5" horizon) could be reached more easily there, than in the central part of the mound (because of its higher absolute elevation)[9] or in the outer slopes of the mound (because of the presence of the city wall).[10] The surface collection of sherds had also revealed a relatively higher

[8]The work was supervised by Mario Liverani, with the assistance of Prof. Lucio Milano, Dr. Barbara Cifola, and Miss Alessandra Asteriti. When the tablets were found, Lucio Milano acted also as epigraphist. In the present report , all the f- and i- numbers refer to the season MZ6 and the area F1.

[9]Area B, cf. G. Buccellati in *Mozan 1*, pp. 59-61 and M. Kelly-Buccellati ibid., pp. 65-66.

[10]Area K, cf. G. Bunnens and A. Roobaert in *Mozan 1*, pp. 61-64; M. Kelly-Buccellati ibid., pp. 67-81.

(though certainly low in absolute terms) presence of Ninevite 5 fragments in the north-western portion of the mound.[11]

Although these assumptions proved to be partly wrong in the course of excavation, area F1 turned out to be particularly interesting for different reasons. The slope of the gully was only partly modelled by erosion, and basically stood on a terraced structure clearly adapted to a slope already existing in the mid-third millennium B.C. It is still possible that, behind and underneath the terraced structure, the Ninevite 5 levels will eventually be reached. For the moment however we are dealing with the same general horizon (metallic/simple ware, although a later variety of each) already met in the central mound (Area B) and in the outer slope (city wall: Area K) which can be dated to the second half of the 3rd millennium.

2.2 Stratigraphy of area F1

The general stratigraphy of area F1 is rather simple (Fig. 3). The materials have not yet been completely studied, however; even the excavation itself is still to be continued in order to reach satisfactory results. We can provide here only a few preliminary and quite general comments, in order to place the tablets in their proper archaeological context.

The upper strata,[12] consisting of washed down materials, to an average depth of ca. 50-60 cm., follow the incline of the present slope. Quite clearly they accumulated in the absence of containing structures, so that no horizontal stratification is present. These layers, although unstratified (and also notably degraded by deep roots and rodents holes), cover a long period of time: most probably extending from the beginning of the 2nd millennium B.C. up until modern times. Some burials (f 15, 26, 28, 81) had been dug in this upper layer, at various depths; at the bottom are a couple of crescent-like stone structures (f 100, 126), the probable remains of huts or shelters, partly cut into the slope.

Under these layers and structures which follow the incline of the present slope, other strata follow which are horizontal in deposition, and are connected to or based upon a terraced structure which gives the slope its present outline (and is

---

[11]M. Kelly-Buccellati in *Mozan 1*, p. 44. Also obsidian fragments are more frequently met in the same area.

[12]Features 95, 10, 19, 11, 16 in the section published as Fig.3.

in its turn most probably containing and regularizing an earlier slope). The terrace wall is built up of a mud-brick core (f 70, 115), with an outer revetment in stone (f 31, 75) towards the "down-stairs" rooms, and an inner pisée fill (f 68) covered with stones (f 30, 67, 82) leveling the "up-stairs" area.

The architectural and stratigraphic interpretation of the "down-stairs" area (north-east of the retaining wall) is quite easy. A line of two store-rooms (f 77 and 125) lies adjacent to, and is protected by, the terrace wall. A second line probably of kitchen rooms (f 129 and 130) lies further north and is still unexcavated (but the tops of two tannurs, f 87 and 128, already appear). The two store-rooms have been excavated down to the floors: one completely (f 93 is the floor of f 77), the other only in part (f 123 is the floor of f 125). They contain a full collection of ceramic vessels, all of them in situ on the floors or benches, and sealed under the burnt collapse of roof and walls.

The interpretation of the "up-stairs" area (south and west of the retaining wall) is more complex. As already mentioned, the space between the earlier slope and brick wall had been filled with bricky material and a row of stones. Behind them, a compacted horizontal layer (f 73), of notable thickness, is probably to be interpreted as the original levelling (floor plus subfloor[13]) of the upper terrace – possibly an open area. Above such a compact layer, some stone structures have been built (f 56+57, 27+29, 59), which cannot be satisfactorily understood before the dig is extended further south. They should belong to a slightly later period than the building of the terraced structure (retaining wall plus f 73); but to a period when the store-rooms (f 77 and 125) were still in use. The same destruction should have affected at the same time both the "upper" structures and the "lower" store-rooms. As far as we know at present (most of f 73 is still to be cleared), the upper floor had no vessels resting on it, and contained very few sherds. For the moment its date is therefore partly dependent on that of the store-rooms, but it is to be hoped that a second campaign in F1, by enlarging the dig southwards, will provide the necessary elements for an independent dating.

---

[13]The compact layer is ca. 50 cm. thick; in the section published here (Fig. 3) f 73 is properly the floor, f 108 the sub-floor.

2.3 The ceramic horizon

In the two storerooms protected by the retaining wall, a large number of vessels have been found in situ on the floors and on the benches: about 50 in f77 and about 15 in the excavated portion of f125. A large repertory of types and sizes is present: large storage jars, medium and small jugs, a variety of goblets and bowls, as well as some stone tools.

A careful study of this material has, of course, to be postponed until the excavation is completed (possibly in the 1992 campaign), the vessels have been fully restored and drawn, and some analysis has been carried out. For the moment, a preliminary examination of a part of the vessels (the large jars are still to be restored) points to a late metallic ware horizon. The best parallels are provided by the so-called "Akkadian" levels in Tell Brak[14], and also in other sites of the Upper Habur area, such as Chaghar Bazar and Tell Leilan – while sites (like Tell Khuera) occupied only to the end of the ED III period, provide a different picture. It is true that some forms in the ceramic inventory of f 77 + 125 go back to earlier traditions[15]. But on the other hand the large jars, with their wavy lines and rope decoration, seem to point to later developments. All in all, a date in the Akkadian period seems to fit best with our material, at least at this preliminary stage of our study. In comparison to the other areas already excavated in Mozan, F1 f 77 + 125 is clearly later than the ED III burnt deposit (f 16) of area K[16], and should be located in between the early floor (ED III) and the later laminations (Ur III) of the stone founded temple in area B.[17]

Apart from the ceramic inventory of f 77 + 125, found in situ on the floors, more pottery fragments were obviously found in the accumulation above both the lower storerooms (f 23 + 32 in the section of Fig. 3) and the upper area (f 37 + 47 in the same section). A few sherds were also found in the very small part of f 73 already removed. All this material, although necessarily mixed and in secondary

[14]Cf. K. Fielden, *Iraq* 39 (1977), pp. 245-255; J. Oates, *Iraq* 44 (1982), pp. 205-219; more "Akkadian" material has been found in the last seasons.

[15]In particular a large jug (i 114) has good parallels in ED III Brak (*Iraq* 44 (1982), p. 209: 4 and 17) and Khuera (H. Kühne, *Die Keramik vom Tell Chuera*, Berlin 1976, Abb. 31 and 35); and an incised jug (i 137) goes back to a form belonging to the "fine, no III) in Leilan (G.M. Schwartz, *A Ceramic Chronology from Tell Leilan*, I, New Haven 1988, fig. 47: 4).

[16]M. Kelly-Buccellati, *Mozan 1*, pp. 66-67.

[17]Ibid., p. 65.

emplacement, belongs quite consistently to the same "late metallic ware" horizon, with very few earlier or later inclusions. But an inner chronology of such material is largely dependent on the recovery of well-sealed primary emplacements like that of the storerooms.

2.4 The findspot of the tablets

The two tablets i 121 and i 122 were found together, inside f 73, the compact layer referred to previously (Illustr. 3.).Their horizontal position (as marked in Fig. 2) is not far from the head of a stone wall (f 82) belonging to the upper arrangement of the terraced structure. The two tablets (and a broken goblet, i 119, in upside-down position) were partly covered by two large fragments of jars (i 108) (Illustr. 9). No trace of a pit was visible, and the soil including the tablets was quite hard, so the possibility that we are dealing with a later inclusion in the already existing compact floor can be ruled out.

It is to be acknowledged that this arrangement of the tablets is not devoid of problems: during excavation the possibility was duly taken into account, that the tablets had been intentionally buried and covered with the jar fragments. But the impression is clearly that the two tablets (and the broken goblet) had been already discarded when included in the floor/sub-floor f 73. Also, the jar fragments were not properly covering them, and their association is the result of pure chance. Most of the area in which the compact layer f 73 extends is remains to be cleared and eventually removed in order to ascertain whether more discarded material is embedded in the floor and sub-floor.

Although the work is still in progress and further clarification will certainly be obtained in the next campaign (by completing the excavation of the entire building), we decided to publish immediately the tablets and their provisional stratigraphic context. It is already certain that the tablets belong to an "Akkadian" level; their more precise relation to the storerooms and their well datable ceramic inventory will be more exactly described in the final report. For the moment, the tablets seem to belong to the *construction phase* of the terraced structure (provided that they are included into f 73, and that f 73 is the original floor of the upper terrace): in this case, they should be (slightly?) earlier than the ceramic inventory of the storerooms, belonging to their *destruction phase.*

3. Philological presentation – L. Milano

3.1 Introduction

The two Old Akkadian cuneiform tablets presented in this article[18] are the first epigraphical documents found in a well-stratified context at Tell Mozan since the beginning of the archaeological excavations at the site in 1984. In spite of their being fragmentary and rather poor in content, the two documents are of the greatest significance, especially considering the very limited amount of textual material dating back to the 3rd millennium B.C., coming from the Upper Khabur region.

In fact, information about this area during the Sargonic and Ur III periods is necessarily based more on archaeological than on written sources. The only available written records from this region are a few Old Akkadian cuneiform inscriptions (on bricks, bullae and clay tablets) from Tell Brak and Chagar Bazar,[19] recovered in the course of regular excavations, and some other documents coming from private dealers, whose origin is still a matter of discussion.

The small group of Old Akkadian inscriptions recovered during Mallowan's excavations at Brak[20] has been increased recently by new and interesting

[18]I wish to thank Profs. Prof. M. Kelly-Buccellati and G. Buccellati – Directors of the Archaeological Excavation at Mozan – for entrusting me with the publication of the tablets dealt with in this article. I am particularly indebted to Profs. A. Westenholz and B. Foster who gave me their advice about the texts and provided me with various suggestions.

[19]Only two Old Akkadian iscriptions (A.391 and A.393) were found by Mallowan at Chagar-Bazar: see C.J. Gadd, *Iraq* 4 (1937), pp. 178 and 185, Pl. XIIIb. (Copy of A.391 also in *AOAT* 3/1, No. 68).

[20]For an up-to-date list of these inscriptions – part of which have been published by C.J. Gadd in *Iraq* 7 (1940), pp. 60-61 and by O. Loretz in *AOAT* 3/1 (Nos. 69-82) – see I.L. Finkel, *Iraq* 47 (1985), pp. 199-201. Except for two tablets, which are still intact, the rest of the texts are fragmentary. Most of them are administrative texts and lists of commodities; in addition, there are some school texts (see A. Westenholz, *AfO* 25 [1974-77], p. 105 f.) and some inscriptions on bullae. Royal

epigraphical finds from the same site, consisting mainly of economic and administrative texts.[21]

The documents bought on the antiquities market would be extremely important, were it not for the lack of data about their archaeological context, common to all of them. They are the seal of Daguna (written in Akkadian),[22] and the famous Hurrian text with the dedication of a temple to the god Nergal by the king of Urkish, Tish-atal (*Ti-iš-a-tal en-dan Ur-kèš*[ki]).[23] The provenance of the lion sculptures on which the inscription was engraved is unknown, but Tell Mozan has been suggested recently as the best candidate.[24] If the Tish-atal inscription dates to the Ur III period, as generally accepted, it would be slightly later than the other important text mentioning a king of Urkish, the so called "Samarra tablet,"[25] probably belonging to the end of the Sargonic period or to the beginning of the Gutean period.[26]

inscriptions of Rimush and Naram-Sin were also found at Tell Brak. For Rimush, see *AOAT* 3/1, No. 83, a fragment belonging to the same inscribed alabaster vase published by M.E.L. Mallowan, *Iraq* 9 (1947), pp. 27, 66, 197, Pl. L, No. 4. (Cf. Finkel's notice at p. 201. Contra: *FAOS* 7, p. 68). As for Naram-Sin, see the several mudbricks stamped with his name, a list of which is provided by Finkel, *ibid.*, pp. 189-190.

[21]See I.L. Finkel, *Iraq* 47 (1985), p. 189-191; I.L. Finkel, *Iraq* 50 (1988), p. 83; N.J.J. Illingworth, *Iraq* 50 (1988), pp. 87-99. Besides 12 texts (or text fragments) on clay tablets, there is also a clay impression of the seal belonging to the ensi of Gasur, and 2 bricks bearing the stamped name of Naram-Sin (to be added to the other five discovered during Mallowan's excavation: see previous note).

[22]This cylinder seal, belonging to Daguna, a wet-nurse (ama-ga-kú), was published by J. Nougayrol, *Syria* 37 (1960), pp. 209-214. For a revised interpretation of the inscription, see P. Steinkeller, *N.A.B.U.* 1988, p.32, *contra* W.G. Lambert, *OA* 26 (1987), pp. 13-16. According to a statement of the dealer (whose opinion is shared with no criticism by Nougayrol) the object had the same origin as the "Lion of Urkish" acquired by the Louvre (see next footnote).

[23]The text is known from the stone tablet and the plaque held by a bronze lion figurine, now at the Louvre Museum (see A. Parrot - J. Nougayrol, *RA* 42 [1948], pp. 1-20; most recently *FAOS* 7, p. 382 with bibl.); and from a parallel and very corrupted version contained on the plaque of a twin lion, now at the Metropolitan Museum (see W. Muscarella in *Mozan 1*, pp. 93-99 with bibl.). Both artifacts have been bought from the same dealer on the antiquities market.

[24]See G. Buccellati in *Mozan 1*, pp. 36-38.

[25]Bronze tablet mentioning Atal-shen, king of Urkish and Nawar, and his dedication of a temple to the god Nergal "king of Khawilum": see F. Thureau-Dangin, *RA* 9 (1912), pp. 1-4 and, more recently, *FAOS* 7, p. 383.

[26]The origin of an independent Hurrian city-state at Urkish has been viewed by G. Wilhelm 1982, p. 13 as a direct consequence of the collapse of the Akkad empire.

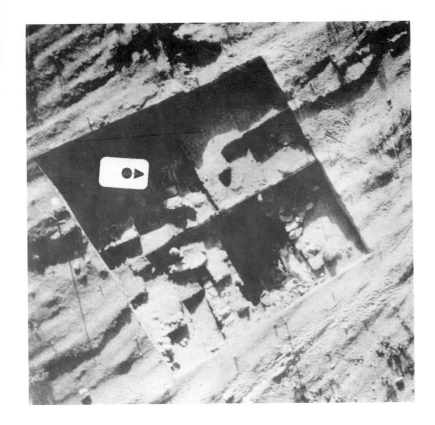

Illustr. 1

**F1: General overhead
of entire unit**

(The symbol ●▶ shows the
location of the tablets)

Illustr. 3

**Close-up
of locus with tablets**

Illustr. 2

**F1: Closer view
of Western portion
of unit**

Plate II   L. Milano *et al.*   [*SMS* 5/1

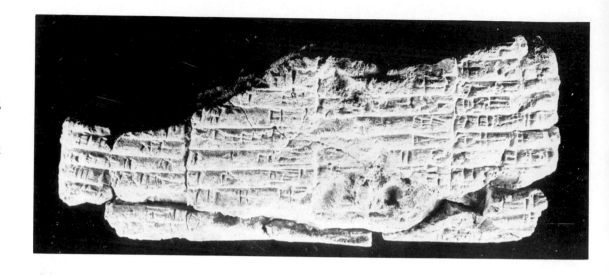

Illustr. 4

M2 1
Obverse (?) of tablet

Illustr. 5

M2 1
Reverse (?) of tablet

Illustr. 6

M2 3
Inscribed sherd

Illustr. 7

M2 2
Obverse of tablet

Illustr. 8

M2 2
Reverse of tablet

Illustr. 9

**Sherds (F1.108) covering
tablets M2 1 and 2 in situ**

(note globlet fragment F1.119,
and stone wall F1f82 on the right)

Illustr. 10

**M2 1-2 in situ
with goblet fragment F1.119**

Illustr. 11

**M2 1-2 in situ
after removal of
goblet fragment F1.119**

These being the limits of our sources, the new Old Akkadian texts from Mozan add some important elements to the reconstruction of the earliest history of the Khabur region: on the one hand they confirm the spread of the Old Akkadian writing tradition in a peripheral area of the empire; on the other hand, they raise the interesting question of the relationship between the local culture such as it is documented by the Hurrian inscriptions attested so far, and the influence of an Akkadian linguistic and cultural milieu, certainly implying an interaction of different ethnic groups.

3.2 Description of the tablets

M2 1 (MZ6, F1.121; see Illustr. 4-5 and Figure 6) is a large fragment of an unbaked tablet measuring 11.8 (width) x 5,1 (height) cm. Its thickness is 2.8 cm in the center and 1.5 cm at the bottom of the face where the script is still preserved. One of the two faces (maybe the reverse?) is in fact completely lost: only a few traces of wedges are visible on the surface, along with some of the lines delimiting columns and cases. It cannot be ascertained if this face was originally convex or flatter than the other one, as it is now, after the break. The text is subdivided into four columns of writing.

M2 2 (MZ6, F1.122; see Illustr. 7-8 and Figures 4-5), is better preserved than M2 1. It measures 8.4 (width) x 7 (height) cm and the two faces are equally convex, the center being thicker (2.4 cm) than the edges (1.6 cm). This tablet, which is also unbaked, is written on both faces, each one divided up into three columns. The obverse is much eroded on the edges, while the central column is in better condition. On the upper and lower part of this column there are two holes (maybe worm holes?), perfectly circular in shape, which go very deep and cut both the cuneiform signs and the horizontal lines that define the cases. The upper hole pierces the tablet, and comes out on the lower edge of the reverse, along an oblique line. The reverse of the tablet is rather well preserved; the writing ends at about the middle of the last column.

3.3 Texts in transliteration

M2 1 (F1.121); see copy on Fig. 6 and photographs on Plate II.

Obv.?	I.	(beginning is missing)	
	1'.	[...] ⌜x⌝	[ ]
		⌜x⌝ ⌜LA⌝ ⌜AK⌝	[ ]
	3'.	ki *Be-lum-a-ḫi*	at the disposal of Belum-aḫi
		ù Ú-[n]a-ap-šè-ni	and Unap-šenni
		[...]	[ ]
	6'.	[...] DA	[ ]
		[...] ⌜x⌝ simug	[ ] the smith
		[...] x	[ ]
	II.	(beginning is missing)	
	1'.	[...] ⌜x⌝	[ ]
		[1?] TÚG.DU₈	the upholsterer:
	3'.	10+5 guruš	15 workmen.
		nu-bànda *I-ti*[-x]	The inspector (is) Iddin-[ ],
		a-zu₅	the physician.
	6'.	*šu* SAL.SILA₄	...
		šu-nígin 60+4 gur[uš]	Total: 64 workmen
		KI [x]	[ ]
	III.	(beginning is missing)	
	1'.	[... gu]ruš	[work]men
		[...] ⌜x⌝ BU	[ ]
	3'.	[...] LUM	[ ]
		[x] ⌜x⌝ NI	[ ]
		[x-x]-*a-ḫi*	[ ]-aḫi
	6'.	[...] UM	[ ]
		[...]	[ ]
		[...] ⌜x⌝	[ ]

IV.   (beginning is missing)

    1'.   [x] DA [x]   [   ]

        Gi-bu-[x]   Gibu[   ],

    3'.   ki NAGAR?.ŠEŠ?   at the disposal of ...;

        Íl-ᒥeᒧ-um   Ilʾeum,

        ki *Šè-ni-za-sa-am*   at the disposal of Šenni-zasam;

    6'.   Im-lu-lu   Imlulu,

        ki [(x-)]ku-da   at the disposal of [ ]kuda;

        šu-nígin 40+[n guruš] Total: 40+[n workmen],

    9'.   [ki? x-b]*ù-n*[*i*]   [at the disposal of?   ]buni.

        [...] A?   [   ]

        ᒥxᒧ ᒥxᒧ [...]   [   ]

M2 2 (F1.122); see copy on Figs. 4-5 and photographs on Plate III.

Obv.   I. 1.   ZI ᒥxᒧ ᒥxᒧ   [   ]

               [...]   [   ]

        3.   [...]   [   ]

               KI [...]   [   ]

               KI? A ᒥxᒧ ᒥxᒧ   [   ]

        6.   [...]   [   ]

               (broken)

   II. 1.   [x-x]-*a?-ḫi*   [   ]-aḫi

               [...]   [   ]

        3.   [...]   [   ]

               [x x] NE x   [   ]

               1? ᒥIm?ᒧ-lu-ᒥluᒧ?   Imlulu (?),

        6.   1? *Ša-lim-a-ḫu*   Šalim-aḫu.

               šu-nígin 10+3 guruš Total: 13 workmen.

               nu-bànda Ì-lu-lu? The inspector (is) Ilulu.

        9.   [1?] Nita-zi   Nitazi (is)

               [l]*ú?*-ŠID x   the accountant (?).

		[x] ⌈x⌉ BE	[ ]
		(broken)	
III.	1.	I ⌈x⌉ [x]	[ ]
		[...]	[ ]
	3.	NA [x]	[ ]
		[x] KI ⌈x⌉	[ ]
		⌈x⌉ [...]	[ ]
	6.	AL? [...]	[ ]
		⌈x⌉ LU [...]	[ ]
		[...]	[ ]
	9.	[...]	[ ]
		[...]	[ ]
		[...]	[ ]
	12.	⌈x⌉ [...]	[ ]
		(broken)	
Rev. IV.	1.	[...]	[ ]
		1? *Sa*-[...]	[ ]
	3.	ì[R- ...]	[ ]
		Sá-ha-⌈x⌉	Saha[ ]
		(empty)	
	6.	1 *Na-bí*-[x]	Nabi[um (?)]
		in Si-⌈x⌉[(x)^{ki}]	in (the village of) Si[ ];
		1 dub-sa[r]	the scribe,
	9.	1 azl[ag?]	the ful[ler] (?)
		[x] ⌈x⌉ [x]	[ ]
		in A-[x(-x)]^{ki}	in (the village of) A[ ];
	12.	[x] SAG ⌈x⌉	[ ]
		1 *Šu-pa-è*	Šupae,
		1 mušen-dù	the fowler,
V.	1.	[...]	[ ]
		[...-*d*]*a*^{ki}	[in (the village of)]da;
	3.	[1?] *A-bù-am*	Abuam,

	1 Ì-lu-lu	Ilulu,
	1 *Ik-su-tum*	Ikšudum,
6.	1 [N]*i-se*$_{11}$*-e-ni-su*	Niši-ēnišu
	in Ar-za-[k]um^{ki}	in (the village of) Arzakum.
	1 *Zi-ra*	Zira,
9.	ki *I-sar-sa-ma-ak*	at the disposal of Išar-samak;
	1 *Gal-bum*	Kalbum,
	[1] ᵓ*À*-WA-*tu-rí*	ᵓAwa-turi,
12.	1 Ab-ba-˺*i-lí*˺	Abi-ili
	KI [x]	[ ]

VI.		(2-3 lines are missing)	
	1'.	[x g]iš-kin-[t]i	[ ] workshop
		in ˹*Da*˺-*aḫ*^{KI}	in (the village of) Dāḫ.
		(rest of the column is empty)	

3.4 Palaeography

The type of writing documented by these two texts fits in with the general features of the Old Akkadian cuneiform script. The signs show, however, a rather cursive and unelegant shape very similar to that of many administrative texts of the time of Sharkalisharri and after. If compared with the Old Akkadian tablets from Tell Brak, the ductus of the Mozan texts appears looser, and many signs, instead of being deeply engraved, arc only superficially scratched. In broad terms, however, the chronological setting should be the same: notice e.g. the signs ŠU and DA, which are drawn with the vertical wedge going downwards, as is typical of the majority of the Akkadian inscriptions later than the time of Sargon. Notice also the shape of GAL, with more than five short horizontal wedges in front of the vertical one.

With regard to the cuneiform rendering of the numerals, a difference seems to exist between the Mozan and Brak inscriptions: in the tablets from Mozan the numerals are consistently rendered by means of wedges, while in those from Tell Brak they are mostly rendered in round form, whether they are used in the accounting of people,[27] or for expressing measures. It is to be acknowledged, however, that most of the numerals attested in the tablets from Tell Brak refer to weight or capacity measures, which are absent, instead, from the two texts from Mozan. On the other hand, pointed number signs are not completely lacking in the Old Akkadian inscriptions from Tell Brak.[28]

A general statement can therefore be made that the tablets from Tell Mozan are contemporary with (or only slightly later than) the Old Akkadian tablets from Tell Brak, i.e. they belong to the latter portion of the Sargonic period. It is actually difficult to suggest a more precise chronology, dealing with a cuneiform tradition imported from Mesopotamia to a peripheral area of the empire, where the availability of written sources is scanty for comparative purposes.

3.5 Content and structure of the texts

Both inscriptions M2 1 (F1.121) and M2 2 (F1.122) deal with the accounting of people (guruš) listed by names, by professions and sometimes by provenience. Personal names in No. 2 are regularly preceded by a vertical wedge.

The list of M2 1 is badly damaged, but the structure of the text is clear enough: in the extant portion of the accounting we have two totals of men (II 7' and IV 8') seemingly put at someone's disposal. The sequence PN_1 ki PN_2, occurring several times in col. IV (see also I 2'-4'), possibly denotes that PN_1 is at the dependence (or at the disposal) of PN_2.[29]

M2 2 is better preserved, at least on the reverse, and does not deserve many comments. Notice that the name of the nu-bànda, "inspector," mentioned in II 7 is not the same as in No. 1 II 4'. The term lú-ŠID has been interpreted as a profession, but it is also attested as a personal name: see *USP*, p. 29 f.

Four place names occur in the text, all preceded by the preposition *in*: two of them are partially broken (see IV 7 and V 2), while the other two names (V 7:

[27]See e.g. *AOAT* 3/1 69; *Iraq* 47 (1985), p. 190 (No. 5).

[28]Cf. *Iraq* 50 (1988), p. 96 (No. 19) and p. 98 (No. 21).

[29]For the sequence PN_1 ki PN_2 in Sumerian lists of personnel of the Sargonic Period, see e.g. B.R. Foster, *VO* 6 (1986), p. 42 and Pl. X (No. 18, from Umma), *RTC* 91 and 93; cf. *ITT* I 1379 Obv. 4-6, *ITT* II/2 5853 Obv. 5-7, *ITT* V 9303.

Ar-za-[k]um^{ki} and VI 2': ^r*Da*¹-*aḫ*^{ki}) probably identify small villages and are not attested elsewhere.[30]

The final expression giš-kin-ti *in* GN, "workshop in (the village of) GN" (VI 1'-2'), possibly refers to the entire group of people listed in the record, whose number is lost in the break at the beginning of col. VI.

3.6 Notes on the personal names

The inventory of personal names attested in our texts is not large, but it is especially interesting with regard to their ethnic distribution. Along with a majority of Akkadian names we find some Hurrian names and other names whose linguistic affiliation is not clear. A list of references and comparative material selected from the Old Akkadian text corpus is provided hereafter.

ʾ*À-WA-tu-rí* (**M2 2** V 11). Hurrian name. Both elements /aw(a/i)-/ and /tur(a/i/u)-/ are well attested at Nuzi (see *NPN*, p. 208a and p. 269b f.; *AAN*, p. 38 and 151 f.). For the Hurrian element /-turi/ see also references at Gasur (*HS*, p. 53), at Mari (Sasson, *Assur* 2/2 [1979], p. 16) and Ugarit (*PTU*, p. 266). On the other hand, no occurrence of a name such as ʾAwa-turi is documented yet in the Hurrian onomastics.

A-bù-am (**M2 2** V 3). I do not know of other occurrences of this name.

Ab-ba-ì-lí (**M2 2** V 12). The logographic spelling for *abum* is rare in Old Akkadian names: see *MAD* 3, p. 11.

Be-lum-a-ḫi (**M2 1** I 3'). Cf. *Be-lí-a-aḫ*: *MAD* 3, p. 22.

Gal-bum (**M2 2** V 10). See *MAD* 3, p. 145. "Dog (of DN)": cf. *Ga-la-ab-É-a* (*ibid.*), *Gal-bù-Aš-dar* (*OSP* 1, 47 I 3).

Gi-bu-[x] (**M2 1** IV 2'). Akkadian name?

I-sar-sa-ma-ak (**M2 2** V 9). The element *sa-ma-ak* can hardly be explained from *samākum*.

---

[30]For a list of place names attested in the Old Akkadian texts from Tell Brak, see particularly *AOAT* 3/1, 69 and N.J.J. Illingworth, *Iraq* 50 (1988), pp. 88-89.

Ik-su-tum (**M2 2** V 5). "He (the new born) has arrived." Also attested as *Ik-šu-tum*: see *MAD* 3, p. 154

Íl-ᵉ¹-um (**M2 1** IV 4'). See *MAD* 3, p. 158; *CAD* L, p. 154b and *AHw*, p. 547b s.v. *leʾū*.

Ì-lu-lu (**M2 2** II 8; V 4). Very common name in the Sargonic sources: see e.g. the list of references in *MAD* 1, p. 204 and *MAD* 5, p. 107.

Im-lu-lu (**M2 1** IV 6'; **M2 2** II 5 ?). The reading of the two last signs is clear (not Im-ku-ku!). The interpretation of the name is however problematic, both in Akkadian and Sumerian.

Na-bí-[x] (**M2 2** IV 6). Possibly *Na-bí-[um]*, since in the break there is room for no more than one sign. For this name, see *MAD* 3, p. 195; Foster, *Or* 51 (1982), p. 341.

Ni-se₁₁-e-ni-su (**M2 2** V 6). "The chosen one" (lit. "The raising of his eyes"). See *MAD* 3, p. 209; Foster, *Or.* 51 (1982), p. 343; Illingworth, *Iraq* 50 (1988), p. 92 (Tell Brak). Cf. *CAD* N₂, p. 296b.

Nita-zi (**M2 2** II 9). This would be a Sumerian name if the reading is correct. See *ITT* II/2 4683; *CT* 50 169, 21; *OSP* 2, *passim* (see the Index, p. 198 s.v.). Since Nita-zi is preceded by another sign (not necessarily the mark for a personal name) broken up by a hole on the clay tablet, a different explanation is not to be excluded. The element -zi could also be interpreted as a formative element of a Hurrian personal name.

Sá-ḫa-ᵣx¹ (**M2 2** IV 4). I found no references for either an Akkadian, Hurrian or Sumerian name beginning with these two syllables.

Ša-lim-a-ḫu (**M2 2** II 6). Also attested as *Sá-lim-a-ḫu* and *Ša-lim-a-ḫu-um*: see *MAD* 3, p. 272.

Šè-ni-za-sa-am (**M2 1** IV 5'). Hurrian name, according to the first element *šè-ni*. As for the element *za-sa-am*, I don't find any good parallel or explanation. Cf. however the name *I-sar-ni-se₁₁-sa-am* in *MAD* 5, 9 I 13 (listed in *MAD* 3, p. 315 *sub I-sar-ni-ḫi-sa-am* as "possibly Akkadian").

Šu-pa-è (**M2 2** IV 13). The interpretation of this name is problematic. Both elements /šu-/ and /-pae(/i)/ are attested in the Hurrian onomastics: see

NPN, p. 242 and 258b. Consider also the occurrence of *šu¹-pa-e* in *ChS* I/1 41 II 43 (šu-u-pa-e: IV 13; šu-u-pa-a-e: IV 19, 20) and the name Šupaya at Nuzi (*NPN*, p. 259b; *AAN*, p. 132b). However, one would expect *Šu-pa-e*, instead of *Šu-pa-è*. An alternative explanation, such as *Šu-pa-è* "He (the god) is manifest"?, on the ground of the Sumerian pa-è (cf. Lugal-pa-è, Íd-pa-è or LUGAL.GI-pa-è "Šarru-kīn is manifest"), seems more difficult.

Ú-na-ap-šè-ni (**M2 1 I 4'**). Hurrian name already known – besides Nuzi (see *NPN* p. 164b; *AAN*, p. 157b) and Alalakh (*AlT*, p. 150) – from Ur III and earlier sources. Cf. *Ú-na-ap-šè-na*: *OSP* 1 47 V 4; *Ú-na-ap-še-in* (on Ur III cylinder seals): *HS*, p. 112 and note 48; *Ú-na-ap-šè-in*: *MAD* 2, p. 110. Both elements /unap-/ and /-šenni/ frequently occur in the Hurrian onomastics in various combinations (see e.g. *NPN*, p. 272b and p. 255b f.; *ShT*, p. 69; *PTU*, p. 250 f.). Note the writing SI-en for /šen/ in the name *A-tal-SI-en* (king of Urkish and Nawar) of the "Samarra tablet" (end of the Sargonic period): *FAOS* 7, p. 383.

Zi-ra (**M2 2 V 7**). *MAD* 5, 62, 4; 65, 4; *OSP* 1, 47 III 5. Is *Zi-ra* to be interpreted as a Hurrian name? The element /zir(a/i/u)/ often occurs in the Hurrian onomastics: see e.g. *NPN*, p. 278b; *AAN*, p. 175; Sasson, *Assur* 2/2 (1979), p. 31.

3.7 Conclusions

A first and in some ways obvious conclusion resulting from the study of the two records presented above is that they generally conform to the standard schemes of the Old Akkadian scribal traditions. The language in which the documents are written is plausibly Akkadian, according to the use of the preposition *in* before the place names. The syllabary, as well as the system of accounting and the formal setting of the lists, are typical of the Sargonic period (apart from the infrequent use of the sumerogram ki in the sequence PN_1 ki PN_2), and clearly demonstrate that the cultural influence of the Akkad empire extended farther north than Tell Brak in the Khabur area, with features similar to those already attested in other regions controlled by the Akkadian rulers.

The names of professions occurring in the lists (a-zu$_5$, dub-sar, mušen-dù, nu-bànda, simug, TÚG.DU$_8$) are among the commonest in documents of that kind and period. More interesting is the inventory of personal names, showing a majority of Akkadian personal names (8 names out of 20), some names which can be explained as Hurrian (*Ú-na-ap-šè-ni, Šè-ni-za-sa-am, ᵓA-WA-tu-rí*), or possibly Hurrian (*Šu-pa-è, Zi-ra*), and other names of dubious origin (some of them, however, common in the Sargonic documents). This is insufficient to provide any statistics for the population living in the Upper Khabur area during the Sargonic period; it is however sufficient to date back to the second half of the third millennium B.C., at least, the presence of a Hurrian ethnic element in the region. Moreover, there is only one Hurrian name in the tablets which is also known in later periods (*Ú-na-ap-šè-ni*): such a circumstance allows us to think that some range of differentiation existed between the Hurrian onomasticon of the third and that of the second millennium, which may only be verified by the discovery of additional documents in future excavations.

4. References

AAN   E. Cassin and J.-J. Glassner, *Anthroponimie et anthropologie de Nuzi*, Vol. 1. *Les anthroponimes*, Malibu 1977.

AOAT 3/1 O. Loretz, *Texte aus Chagar Bazar und Tell Brak*, Teil 1, (Alter Orient und Altes Testament, Band 3), Neukirchen-Vluyn 1969.

AlT   D.J. Wiseman, *The Alalakh Tablets*, London 1953.

Börker-Klähn, J.
  1982   *Altvorderasiatische Bildstelen und vergleichbare Felsreliefs*, Mainz.

ChS   I/1 V. Haas, *Die Serien* itkahi *und* itkalzi *des AZU-Priesters, Rituale für Tašmišarri und Tatuhepa sowie weitere Texte mit Bezug auf Tašmišarri* (Corpus der Hurritischen Sprachdenkmler. I. Abteilung: die Texte aus Bogazköy, Band 1), Roma 1984.

CT   *Cuneiform Texts from Babylonian Tablets in the British Museum*, London 1896 ff.

Dossiers   G. Buccellati and M. Kelly- Buccellati, "Tell Mozan," *Les dossiers d'Archéologie* 155 (1990) 18-23.

FAOS 7   I.J. Gelb and B. Kicnast, *Die altakkadischen Königsinschriften des dritten Jahrtausends v.Chr.* (Freiburger Altorientalische Studien, Band 7), Stuttgart 1990.

Fossey, Ch.
  1926   *Manuel d'Assyriologie*, Vol. II, Paris 1926.

HS   I.J. Gelb, *Hurrians and Subarians* (The Oriental Institute of the University of Chicago. Studies in Ancient Oriental Civilization, No. 22), Chicago 1944.

ITT   *Inventaire des tablettes de Tello conservées au Musée Impérial Ottoman*, Paris 1910-1921.

Kelly-Buccellati, M.
  1990a   "Three Seasons of Excavation at Tell Mozan," in S. Eichler, M. Wäfler, D. Warburton, *Tall al-Hamidiya 2*, Orbis Biblicus et Orientalis: Series Archaeologica 6, Göttingen 1990, 119-132.
  1990b   "A New Third Millennium Sculpture from Mozan," in A. Leonard and B. Williams, eds., *Essays in Ancient Civilization Presented to Helene J. Kantor*, SAOC 47, Chicago, 149-54, Pl. 26.

MAD 1   I.J. Gelb, *Sargonic Texts from the Diyala Region* (Materials for the Assyrian Dictionary, No. 1), Chicago 1952.

MAD 2   I.J. Gelb, *Old Akkadian Writing and Grammar* (Materials for the Assyrian Dictionary, No. 2), Chicago 1961^2.

MAD 3   I.J. Gelb, *Glossary of Old Akkadian* (Materials for the Assyrian Dictionary, No. 3), Chicago 1957.

MAD 5   I.J. Gelb, *Sargonic Texts in the Ashmolean Museum, Oxford* (Materials for the Assyrian Dictionary, No. 5), Chicago 1970.

Moortgat, Anton
  1959   *Archäologische Forschungen der Max Freiherr von Oppenheim-Stiftung im nördlichen Mesopotamien 1956*, Köln.

Moortgat, Anton and Ursula Moortgat-Correns
  1976   *Tell Chuera in Nordost-Syrien: Vorläufiger Bericht über die siebente Grabungskampagne 1974*, Berlin.

Mozan 1   G. Buccellati and M. Kelly-Buccellati, *Mozan 1. The Soundings of the First Two Seasons* (Bibliotheca Mesopotamica, Vol. 20), Malibu 1988.

NPN   I.J. Gelb, P.M. Purves and A.A. MacRae, *Nuzi Personal Names* (The University of Chicago Oriental Institute Publications, Vol. 57), Chicago 1943.

Oates, Joan
  1986   "Tell Brak: The Uruk/Early Dynastic Sequence," in Uwe Finkbeiner and Wolfgang Röllig, eds., *Ǧemdat Naṣr Period or Regional Style?*, Wiesbaden.

OSP 1   A. Westenholz, *Old Sumerian and Old Akkadian Texts in Philadelphia Chiefly from Nippur. Part One: Literary and Lexical Texts and The Earliest Administrative Documents from Nippur* (Bibliotheca Mesopotamica, Vol. 1), Malibu 1975.

OSP 2   A. Westenholz, *Old Sumerian and Old Akkadian Texts in Philadelphia. Part Two: The "Akkadian" Texts, the Enlilemaba Texts, and the Onion Archive* (The Carsten Niebuhr Institute Publications, Vol. 3), Copenhagen 1987.

PTU   F. Gröndahl, *Die Personennamen der Texte aus Ugarit* (Studia Pohl, Vol. 1), Roma 1967.

RTC   F. Thureau-Dangin, *Recueil de tablettes chaldéennes*, Paris 1903.

SAB 2   G. Buccellati, G. and M. Kelly-Buccellati, "Tell Mozan," *Syrian Archaeology Bulletin*, 2 (1990), pp. 4-7.

ShT   J. Laessøe, *The Shemshāra Tablets. A Preliminary Report*, København 1959.

USP   B.R. Foster, *Umma in the Sargonic Period* (Memoirs of the Connecticut Academy of Arts and Sciences, Vol. 20), Hamden 1982.

Wilhelm, G.
  1982   *Grundzüge der Geschichte und Kultur der Hurriter*, Darmstadt 1982.

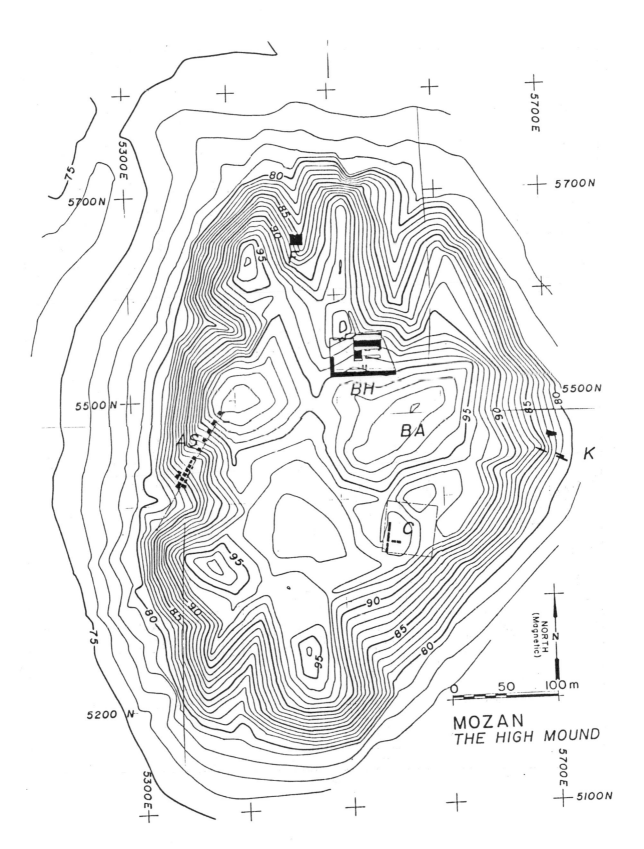

Figure 1
Site plan of Mozan

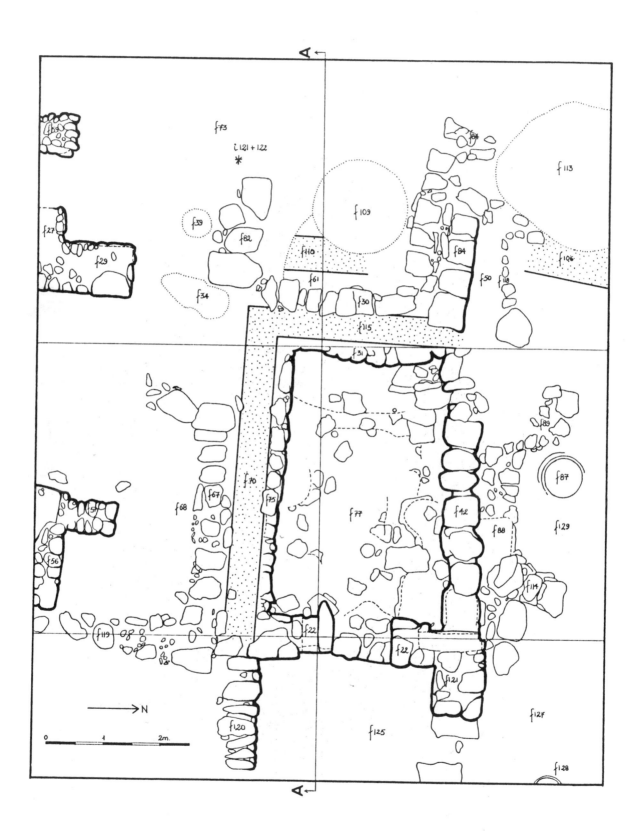

Figure 2
F1: Floor plan

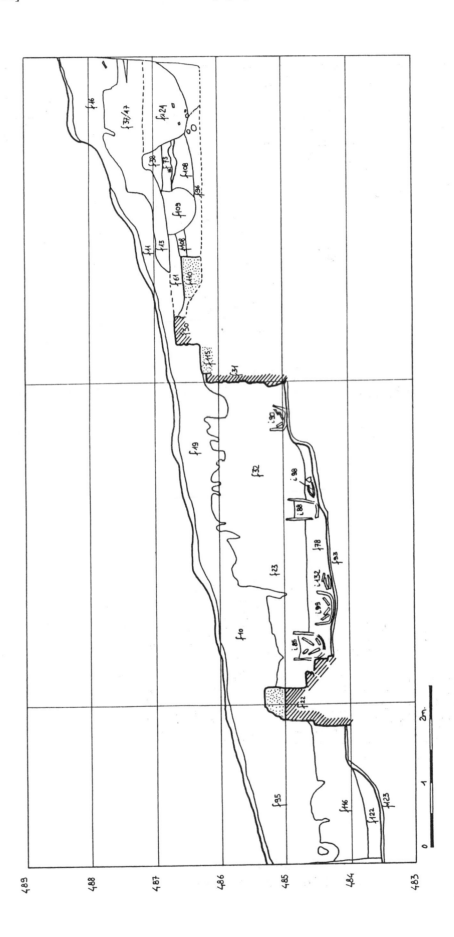

Figure 3
F1: Section AA

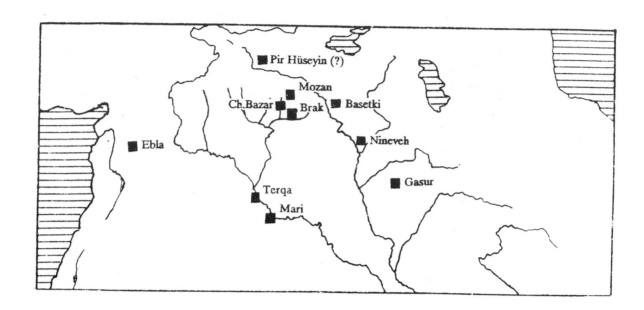

Figure 4
Third millennium epigraphic finds from Northern Syro-Mesopotamian sites

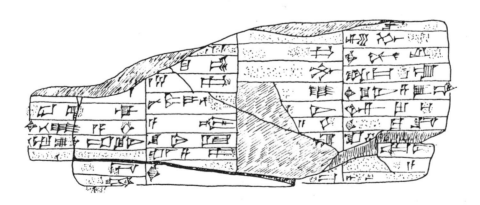

Figure 5
M2 1: Obverse (?) (1:1)

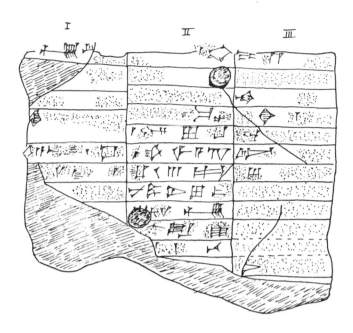

Figure 6
M2 2: Obverse (1:1)

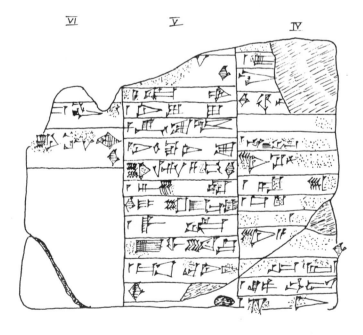

Figure 7
M2 2: Reverse (1:1)

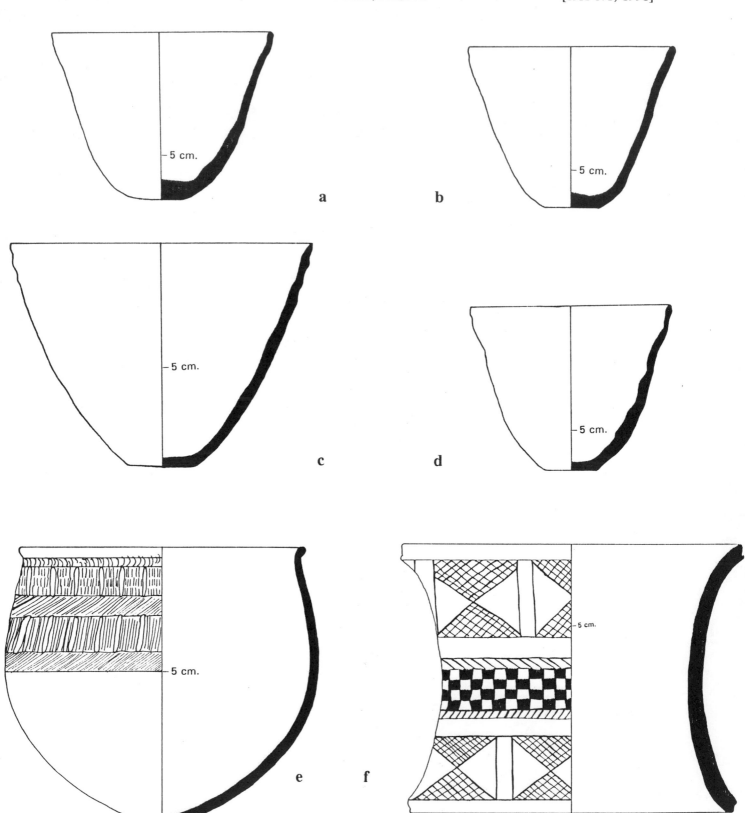

Figure 8
Early third millennium ceramics from grave Ob1

a-d: Metallic ware cups; e: Ninevite V deep bowl; f: Scarlet ware stand
Field numbers: a: Ob1.25; b: Ob1.26; c: Ob1.57; d: Ob1.36; e: Ob1.47; f: Ob1.52